T0266005

THE MILLION DOLLAR SECRET HIDDEN IN YOUR MIND

THE
MILLION DOLLAR
SECRET HIDDEN
IN YOUR MIND

by Anthony Norvell

The Lost Classic on
How to Control Your Thoughts
for Wealth, Power, and Mastery

Abridged and Introduced
by Mitch Horowitz

THE CONDENSED 📖™ CLASSICS LIBRARY™

Published by Gildan Media LLC
aka G&D Media.
www.GandDmedia.com

FIRST EDITION: 2018

Cover design by David Rheinhardt of Pyrographx

Interior design by Meghan Day Healey of Story Horse, LLC.

ISBN: 978-1-7225-0044-3

Contents

A Better Path to Power

You may have noticed a lot of books on attaining power making the rounds lately. Many of them, in my view, are unappealing. They encourage the pursuit of success without nobility, proffering methods like taking credit for other people's efforts or ideas, intimidating acquaintances, withholding information, and being a general sneak.

There is a better way. And it appears in the condensation you are about to experience of an overlooked and underestimated work from 1963: *The Million Dollar Secret Hidden in Your Mind*. Its author, Anthony Norvell, was a jack-of-all-trades success guru who reached his highest watermark with this practical, shrewd, and principled book. In it, Norvell makes memorable and substantive points about the non-exploitative pursuit of worldly success.

Norvell wrote with more edge than a Dale Carnegie, but always with an eye on legitimate personal growth. For example, Norvell pushes you to cultivate influence through the "law of proximity," which means seeking the company of people who encourage your finest traits, provide good examples to emulate or imitate, do not indulge your lowest habits, and challenge you to match them in mental acumen, not in money. Norvell observed how the most retrograde influences in your life are likely to come from "old neighborhood" friends and acquaintances, who forever see you as you were in childhood, and who nudge you toward past, and often dysfunctional, patterns of behavior.

Here are some of my favorite Norvell aphorisms. They may seem elementary but their meaning is deeper than may first appear.

- "Most people have a tendency to minimize themselves and their abilities."
- "To be great, you must dwell in the company of great thoughts and high ideals."
- "Do not be afraid to ask important people to help you."
- "Your subconscious mind will give you valuable ideas, but if you do not write them down, they leave suddenly, and it is difficult to recall them again."

- "Your mind likes *definiteness*. Give yourself a five-year plan for study, growth, and evolvement."
- "You must create a need in your life for the things you want."
- "Determine that you will never use your money for any destructive or degrading act."
- "*Know what you want of life.*"
- "You build your sense of self-importance by studying constantly."

Yes, there are more sophisticated works of mental therapeutics than Anthony Norvell's. You can read the essays of Ralph Waldo Emerson and William James (and you should); you can approach the complex metaphysics of Mary Baker Eddy and Thomas Troward; or you can immerse yourself in the luminous spiritual visions of Neville Goddard and Ernest Holmes. But there exists in Norvell's work a sapling of all those figures. What's more, Norvell writes with a delightful, infectious simplicity.

I often think of how to reply when asked to recommend a single book on mind power. This could be such a book. It is easily digestible and surprisingly broad in scope. You'll enjoy its ideas—but, above all, you must use them. Proof of their depth is in application.

—Mitch Horowitz

CHAPTER ONE

Dynamic Thinkers
Rule the World

A legend is told of the time when the Gods created man and the universe. They held a conference and one of them said, "Let us give man the same creative power that we ourselves possess. Where shall we hide this priceless gift?"

Another answered, "Let us hide it where man will never think to look for it; within his own mind."

And this is where the Million Dollar Secret resides; within your own mind, your own consciousness. Here it is that you can find all the creative power you will ever need to make a fortune or to give yourself a million dollars worth of health, happiness, friendship, love, and enjoyment in life.

The great philosopher Descartes had a philosophy

that can be summarized in one dynamic sentence: "I think, therefore I am."

Dynamic thinking can set into motion a series of reactions that are cataclysmic in their effects.

Ask yourself: "What do I think?" Then answer candidly.

Do you think of yourself as a failure in life?

Do you think you are inferior and inadequate?

Do you think you are doomed to poverty all your life?

Do you think your personality is unattractive?

If you are thinking these negative thoughts, you are short-circuiting the dynamic power of your brain and creating the image of these negative conditions in the outer circumstances of your life. Thoughts are a psychological reality. We each live in a world colored and dominated by our own private thought atmosphere.

Change the picture of your thoughts from negative to positive. Dynamic thinking will cause you to **be** that which you **think**.

Think you are successful.

Think that you are adequate, that you are equal to others.

Think that you can achieve the riches that others have.

Think that your personality may become magnetic and attractive.

You are using the magical power of dynamic thinking in the moment that you think in a positive manner. "I think, therefore I am." Write that down on a card, which you can consult several times daily, and on that card also write, "I think and talk success, health, happiness, and achievement. I think great thoughts, therefore I am great."

CHAPTER TWO

The Undiscovered Genius Within Your Mind

There is a popular expression:

Sow a thought, reap a habit;
Sow a habit, reap a character;
Sow a character, reap a destiny.

Actually you build your future destiny thought by thought, and as these thoughts become more dynamic and perfect, they begin to shape your character and destiny in paths of greatness.

Now you are embarked upon the thrilling voyage of discovery that will lead you to the finding of new worlds, but there are shoals and pitfalls which I must warn you about.

Most of the pitfalls are your own relatives and friends. They have lived with you for many years and have been used to the shrinking violet you may have become under the regime of weak, negative thinking of the past. These friends and relatives feel comfortable in the presence of the small ego that fits their concept of your totality of power. When the slumbering mental giant that is within your mind begins to stir restlessly and tries to shake off the chains that bind it to mediocrity, failure, poverty, and ignorance, these people are apt to set up a clamor that will shock the giant back into his somnolent state of immobility and inertia.

Just remember that every genius of history has had to go through discouragement, often from people close to him, before breaking the bonds of negativity and frustration. A prophet is without honor in his own country, Scripture tells us. Those closest to you are sometimes the very last ones to recognize the genius within you or to give you recognition for having great talent.

Use these three steps to release the undiscovered genius within your mind:

1. Each day try to originate some new and daring concept of thought in relation to your life. Write these down in a notebook and begin to apply them to your activities.

2. Live in your imagination at least one half hour a day. See yourself as the person you wish to be. Visualize yourself as the manager of the department where you work See yourself owning your own business. Imagine yourself taking trips to foreign countries. Build the new concept of your great powers by seeing how many refinements you can make on inventions and technologies. Write down ideas for great stories, novels, movies. You may not intend to be a writer but this mental exercise will extend your thinking to the realm of creative ideas and cause the subconscious mind to release more power to your everyday activities.

3. Pick some outstanding genius of history each day and emulate his philosophy, his thinking, his inspiration. Study the lives of great geniuses of history, searching for great thoughts which you may make a part of your own mental equipment. For instance, Pasteur. Concentrate on his persistence and patience. Edison. Borrow his vision and curiosity, and apply those qualities to your own life, seeing how many things you can mentally create, and how many useful facts you can discover.

CHAPTER THREE

You Are Greater Than You Think

Most people have a tendency to minimize themselves and their abilities. Such people depreciate their own talents, their personalities, and tend to put others on a pedestal.

You cannot achieve a great destiny or a big fortune if you constantly believe yourself inferior and unworthy. Some people have subconscious feelings of guilt, put into their minds by their parents when they were children, and these guilt feelings hound them throughout life, making them unhappy, and dooming them to live lives that are inferior and inadequate. You may have been told that it is wrong and sinful to want to be successful, famous, and rich, and that only the "Meek shall inherit the earth." You must break such negativity at once, and believe *that you are greater than you think*.

The natural intelligence is greater in you than it is in all of nature's other creatures, for you represent the highest form of creation in the universe. When you discover the unlimited realm of the mind you can use it to shape the world you desire. This inner intuitive power that is in every animal, insect, bird and beast, is awaiting your recognition and bidding. When you once discover this power and learn through this study how to channel it correctly, you will be able to achieve seeming miracles in your own life.

Begin today to realize that you live in an unlimited universe, with unlimited resources. There are billions of worlds in outer space and science is now beginning to realize that more worlds are being born every day. The secret power back of all creation is intelligence.

To be great you must dwell in the company of great thoughts and high ideals. Your mind becomes stronger and more intelligent when you pass through it great thoughts, when you desire great things in your life, when you strive for high achievements. To expand your thinking into an area of importance and success, there must be a corresponding degree of inspiration and energy-drive in your thinking. If the idea held in consciousness is big enough, all the actions that follow will be of a like quality and degree.

It takes no more energy mentally to think of a big

job, with good pay, than it does to think of an inferior position with small pay. People will set the value on you and your talents that you set on yourself.

All great men who have ever achieved anything worthwhile or enduring, have been infused with this higher purpose in living. There must be a change in your mental concept first; the idea that you want to express, the work you want to do, the home you want to live in; when you once **know for sure** what it is you want, and you hold tenaciously to that idea, your circumstances of life will gradually begin to change. Do not worry about how this higher mind within you is going to produce the change. You cannot tell this infinite intelligence, which rules the world, how to create an oak tree; this is God's secret. But you can plant the tiny acorn in the soil and then, under the universal laws of growth and capillary attraction, that acorn will attract to itself all the nourishment it needs from the soil and rain, to make a giant oak tree a hundred feet tall.

Do these things to become greater:

1. Build your sum of knowledge. You grow in mental power as your fund of knowledge grows.
2. Learn to crawl before you walk, but try to run as quickly as you gain strength and confidence in your power to walk. In other words, do not remain in a position that is inferior.

3. Make decisions quickly. Do not vacillate after making a decision, but act on your decision promptly.

4. Write to important people presenting your great ideas. Some people have won promotion and success through this process of calling attention to themselves.

5. Do not be afraid to ask important people to help you. They are human and are often flattered to think that you believe they are important enough to give you assistance.

CHAPTER FOUR

Tap the Hidden Treasures Within Your Mind

You may not think your ideas are valuable because they came from your brain. Change your attitude about the value of your thoughts. Some of the greatest things in the world were accomplished by men and women like you, who had just one good idea and made it pay dividends.

When I was lecturing in Honolulu, I met a man at my lectures who had invented the silent mercury switch for electric lights. He had been awakened so many times by the noise of the electric switch when his wife would turn it on at night that his mind began to think of some way to make the turning on of a light switch silent.

Your own ideas may be worth a fortune. You must sit quietly in your own room for at least half-an-hour daily and probe the goldmine of your mind. You should then write down all new ideas that come to you for improving your life, perfecting some product, marketing some merchandise you have created.

Start with whatever field you are in now, and do not wait for some better time or more improved conditions. Look around you, see what could be changed or improved, and then set about doing it. Start this process now and continue it the rest of your life, and you will see amazing results.

Epictetus said, "No great thing is created suddenly, any more than a bunch of grapes or a fig. If you tell me that you desire a fig, I answer you that there must be time. Let it first blossom, then bear fruit, then ripen."

Use this daily regimen for tapping the hidden treasures of your mind:

1. Begin each day, when you waken in the morning, by passing through your mind a series of big ideas relating to your life, your work, your environment. Ask yourself: "What can I do today to improve my situation in life? How can I improve my business? What ideas can I incorporate in my work that will pay me rich dividends in the future?"

2. Check your mind and see if you are using all the power that you possess or if you are wasting it on petty, unimportant things. Could you use more

daring, courage, patience, persistence, thrift, sociability, optimism, humor in your relations with others? Are you using the gifts and talents you possess as steppingstones to greatness? Are you using the knowledge you possess fully? Do you seek the aid of important people you've met to help you achieve your goals?

3. Keep a daily diary in which you jot down each night the outstanding ideas you had during that day. Let your imagination soar without restraint, and carefully note the ideas and suggestions that flash into your mind. Then write them down for future use. Many times your subconscious mind will give you valuable ideas, but if you do not write them down they leave suddenly and it is difficult to recall them again. Edison kept a notebook by his bedside, and his biggest ideas for his many inventions came to him while he slept. He wrote them down at once, and the next day acted on these inspirational ideas.

4. Stir your mind to action by holding in your mind each day a desire to achieve something important and worthwhile. An artist cannot paint his picture until he first has the visual image in his mind. The desire to create that particular picture stirs him into action and he projects his mental picture

onto the canvas before him. You must do the same thing: hold in your mind daily the pictures of the things you wish to achieve. Do not worry how you will attain them. The law of cause and effect takes over the moment you have a strong idea in mind.

CHAPTER FIVE

Magnetism, the Law of Universal Attraction

You can magnetize what you want in life. You must image it mentally; clearly and emotionally, feeling it is already yours. You must write it down. You must visualize the persons, conditions, money, success—whatever it is you want clearly and as often as possible. The process known as daydreaming is helpful in fixing the image clearly in your mind. Daydream yourself in the situations in life you desire, such as singing, speaking or acting. Do the entire performance as if you were actually before that audience. Picture yourself in the job you desire, seeing yourself as an executive, giving orders, having other employees under you. Follow this process based on whatever desires you hold.

Energy and matter are interchangeable. The energy of the mind can be converted into material substance. For instance, the idea to build a bridge is only mental energy, but it can become externalized in the building of the actual bridge. The idea for a painting, a literary work, an invention, or a business is just as real and has a dimension that is as solid and actual as matter. The *idea for a thing* has inherent in it the ability to magnetize the thing itself and bring it into being. This is the way that your mental energy has in itself the equivalent of the thing you are holding in your mind. Be sure then that you magnetize *only* positive things.

The Bible speaks of it as, "As ye sow, so shall ye reap." This is the great mental law of attraction at work in nature.

Take these six steps for greater magnetic power:

1. Picture clearly the things that you want to magnetize and attract. Sit quietly in your room and run these pictures through your mind like film through a movie projector. Review these pictures daily, as often as possible, especially at night just before going to sleep. See them clearly; do *not* keep changing them, but have the pictures the same each time. Have as many things as you want to magnetize, taking them up one at a time, and giving about ten minutes to picturing each thought.

2. Write down the things you wish to magnetize. Write them clearly and briefly. This serves to imprint them on your subconscious more forcibly.

3. Engage in constructive daydreaming when possible. The moments you spend waiting for a car or bus, the time you take out for coffee or a break at work—use these precious moments to daydream. In these daydreams, see yourself as your ideal.

4. *Do not tell anyone* of the secret power you are using. They will tend to laugh at you, discourage you, and they may short-circuit your magnetic attraction with their negative ideas. The acorn grows in the secret, hidden womb of the earth, safe from all interference, and becomes an oak tree because of this secrecy. What if someone tore it up by the roots every few days to see if it was growing? It would die. So, too, your dreams die if they are shattered by others.

5. Have faith in the invisible intelligence that resides in nature to produce the things you are trying to magnetize. The secret power that can make a baby in nine months knows how to release the energy to bring your idea or dream to fruition. But you must have faith in this invisible power that creates all life.

6. Share your good with the world. There is magnetism in giving to others.

CHAPTER SIX

The Magic Genie Within Your Subconscious Mind

In Aladdin's Lamp resided a Magic Genie, who would carry out any wish Aladdin had. All he had to do was rub the magic lamp and the Genie would appear ready to carry out his bidding.

Your subconscious mind might be likened to this Genie. It is ready to carry out any command that you give it. And like the Magic Genie, your subconscious mind is a powerful aid, a dynamic force that can be harnessed for great achievement.

When you see a great pianist like Vladimir Horowitz sit at the piano and play a difficult concerto with such ease and fluency, it is because he has spent years in building the habit patterns of perfection in his mind. The subconscious stores these memoires and releases them under automatic control, so the pianist need not consciously think of how he going to play the difficult score.

All your habit patterns can be built in your subconscious mind so they become automatic responses of your body functions. You can learn how to become a great speaker, writer, composer, musician, inventor, or business success. You may consciously choose the things you want your subconscious to do for you automatically, and then by constant repetition of the act or thought, you will imprint it on your subconscious mind, making it a part of the automatic reflex action of your subconscious.

Modern psychosomatic medicine has shown that one's mental attitude also has much to do with sickness or health. When you constantly repeat positive statements such as, "I am healthy. I am happy. I am young. I have vitality and energy," you actually help raise the energy levels of your body and release the stored sugar in your liver, giving you greater vitality.

The subconscious accepts as truth whatever you tell it often enough. When you repeat an idea over and over again, your subconscious mind automatically accepts it as gospel, and sets to work making it a reality in your life. In psychology, this is known as the Law of Predominant Mental Impression. It simply means that you must keep repeating an idea, saying it over so often that it becomes a law for your subconscious mind.

For instance, if you keep telling yourself, "I can't do that, I'm afraid I'll fail, I'm inferior and inadequate, I'm tired and weak, I'm afraid I'll catch cold," you will make these negative statements the laws of your subconscious mind. As this mind automatically carries out everything you think or say many times, the sympathetic nervous system will set these negative forces into motion. You will become more and more fearful. You will do things that make you fail. You will become inferior. You will be constantly tired and weak. You set the mental stage for the action you imprint upon the subconscious mind.

One of the best ways to reach your subconscious mind and imprint upon it the things you want it to do, is to begin to act the part you wish to play in life. If you want to be rich and successful, act as though you already are. If you want to be happy, begin to act as though you are already happy: smile, be optimistic, talk about the good things of life instead of the sad and evil things. Your subconscious reacts according to the emotional pattern that you set for yourself. If you act happy and successful, your subconscious will send positive pulsations to your glands and the entire rhythm of your body will change to a positive one.

When Napoleon decided he would become Emperor of France, he called in François-Joseph Talma,
one of the nation's leading tragedians, to show him how
to walk, talk, and look like an emperor. Napoleon had a
real problem, for he was scarcely five feet tall. The actor
made him strut back and forth, giving commands as an
emperor would; he showed him how to stand, how to
talk, how to think like an emperor. Finally, when Napoleon was ready to declare himself Emperor Napoleon
the First, he carried such conviction that the crowed
heads of Europe bowed before him.

If you act a part long enough, your subconscious
mind will be impressed by it, and make it living reality. You can begin to achieve a strong, more dynamic
personality by this art of impersonation. Stand before a
mirror and speak to yourself. Tell yourself that you are
strong, dynamic, good looking: really believe the things
you are going to become. Then go around *being* the person you wish to be. Soon, it will become second nature.
You will be guided to doing the things you have long
acted out. People will begin to see you as the person you
have mentally thought yourself to be.

Elsewhere we are told of the importance of writing down your desires and ambitions. Now it is time
for you to know how this simple act works to imprint
upon your subconscious mind the suggestions you write

down. Your subconscious mind believes everything that is repeated to it often enough—things that are said or written down. The kinetic action of *doing* something with your hands more forcibly impresses the subconscious than if you just *think* a thing.

Another great secret for releasing subconscious power is to read or talk aloud. There is something magical about the hypnotic power of the human mind. When you give yourself autosuggestions, and believe what you are telling yourself, you are deeply imprinting the subconscious mind with what you say.

Review these facts for great subconscious power:

1. Turn over the automatic function of your body completely to your subconscious mind. Stop worrying about the way your body works and trust your subconscious to take care of it.

2. Use the system of autosuggestion devised by French mind theorist Emile Coué, and every night just before you drift off to sleep whisper to yourself at least twenty times, "Every day in every way, I am getting better and better." Do the same immediately upon waking in the morning.

3. Memorize other autosuggestions which you repeat every day when you have a few minutes of time, such as, "I can do this job perfectly. I will win a promotion and a raise in salary. I like other people,

and they like me. I can be a big success. I am bigger than I think." You can make up your own suggestions to fit your needs.

4. Write down your main dream or goal at least once a week, and keep where you can see it every day. Keep reviewing it in your mind until it becomes second nature.

5. Sit quietly for ten minutes a day and pass through your imagination mental pictures of yourself doing things you really want to do, such as singing, acting, being in your own business, living in a new house, buying a car, taking a long trip. The important thing is to keep reviewing the picture in detail, until it is such a big part of your consciousness that your subconscious will take it up and act on it.

Chapter Seven

Duplicate the Power of the Great Men of History

When Thomas Edison failed time after time in perfecting his electric light bulb he never stopped trying to find some substance that would last more than a few seconds in the filaments of his lamps. He was so resourceful that he tried thousands of different substances, and each time he failed. But still he did not give up. One day his assistant become so discouraged that he said, "Mr. Edison you've tried ten thousand times and failed, why don't you give up?"

Edison replied, "No, I can't give up. Now we know ten thousand things that won't work." And soon he found something that *did work*.

If you wish to be great and make your fortune, learn how to duplicate the power of the greatest men and women in history. These figures discovered The Million Dollar Secret, some by accident, others through inspiration or sheer dint of hard work and persistent effort.

There are three things that will make you outstanding in any business field, and these three things were present in the works of all geniuses:

1. Ability to know your own talents and possibilities.
2. Daring to attempt the seeming impossible.
3. Courage to persist in the face of obstacles.

The step of determining what you want, and letting your desires guide you to the path you wish to take, is the most important in applying the Million Dollar Secret to your own life and success.

Follow this step-by-step formula to greatness:

1. Pick the field you wish to specialize in; learn all you can about it, study the lives of its outstanding successes, then strive to emulate their pattern of thinking.
2. Each day strive to put into action one or more of the qualities or traits that you have learned from the lives of great men. Imitate these thoughts, if need be, at first, then you will gradually begin to originate great thoughts and actions of your own.
3. Get specialized training to perfect your gifts and talents. Assemble facts about the work you choose;

see the good and bad sides, then, if you remain interested, let no one divert you from your goal.

4. Let what I call Divine Discontent motivate you in your desire to achieve perfection. Never be satisfied with your present accomplishments or progress. When you are satisfied, you cease to grow. Everything in nature is in constant flux, from an imperfect to a more perfect state. Constantly desire change and evolvement.

5. Aim for the stars, even though you may not achieve them; at least such an ambition will assure you of reaching some kind of high goal. Browning said, "Ah, but a man's reach should exceed his grasp, / Or what's a heaven for?"

6. Create a vortex of mental activity about yourself. Break the inertia that may be holding you back by doing *something*, almost anything is preferable to sitting back and refusing to make an effort.

7. Never be satisfied with the limitations that life seems to have placed on you and your expression of your talents. There are means and possibilities all about you—search them out and use them. Part of our Million Dollar Secret is the building of mental power, so you may better express your God-given gifts and talents.

CHAPTER EIGHT

The Million-Dollar Personality That Wins

Some people seem to be born lucky. They grow up in circumstances that seem favorable for their maturing into well-balanced, integrated personalities. They seem to possess charm and attractiveness; everyone seems to like them, and want to help them.

Others are less fortunate. They are born in environments that may be negative and shabby, surrounded by people who are negative, fearful, financially pinched, and constantly worried. These people acquire mental habits that are difficult to break in adult life.

Epictetus said of habit: "Every habit and faculty is preserved and increased by correspondent actions, as the habit of walking, by walking, or running, by running."

The more you practice thinking or doing a thing, the easier it becomes, until finally, by building positive mental habits you are able to perform consistently at a high level of action in the expression of your personality.

It is possible for you now to choose the type of persona you want to be, just as you choose the suit or dress you want to wear. Psychologists tell us that we are conditioned by our own minds through suggestions and opinions we hold, or tell ourselves. If you constantly tell yourself you are inferior, you will gradually begin to take on the hangdog appearance of an inferior person. You will shrink from contact with people. They will sense your reactions and shy away from you.

If you make it a point to reinforce your ego by telling yourself you are worthy of the best life has to offer, and that you are likeable, pleasant, happy, and loving towards others, people will instantly feel your power and gravitate toward you.

Building a magnetic personality is easy when you once know how. It is a matter of satisfaction to be able to win friends and hold them, but it has intrinsic value also that can be counted in actual dollars and cents. Tests given by psychologists proved that men and women who had studied their personalities and worked to perfect and polish them actually got more jobs as executives than those who had inferior personalities but great ability. If it comes to a choice between a pleasant, cheerful, happy-appearing person for a job, and one who is morose and sullen all the time, ability being equal, the pleasant person will be selected every time.

CHAPTER NINE

Ten Steps That Can Make You a Mental Giant

B efore you begin your study of this part of the Million Dollar Secret, I ask that you rid your mind of all doubts and uncertainties, and do *really believe you can do the things I am going to tell you about.* Remove the shadows of fear and doubt and limitation that may fill your mind, and then become imbued with only one thought: *you can do anything you desire!*

Make these ten steps part of your life:

1. **Listen to the Master Mind within.** There is a vast intelligence in all of nature that regulates and operates the entire universe. This Master Mind also works through your own mind; if you learn how tap its power you will have increased your mental capacity at least fifty percent. See how this Master

Mind works in nature. The maple tree produces seed that the Master Mind has given wings, like a parachute. Why wings? Because this Intelligence *knows* that if maple seeds fall in the shade of the mother tree they will have little chance to survive, so they have wings that the wind can catch and blow to a sunny patch of ground. This Intelligence leaves nothing to chance to assure the success and perpetuity of her creation; she gives the maple tree literally thousands of winged seed, to be sure that some of them will survive the caprices of Fate. Learn to listen to the Master Mind within. Be in tune with it; it wants your success and happiness *more than you do!*

2. **Expand your thinking to encompass broader fields of experience and action.** Most people limit themselves to habit-patterns of thought that include their small, everyday happenings. They never allow themselves to soar into the unlimited world of creative thought where they envision wonderful experiences, better jobs, bigger income, the accumulation of a fortune. The habit patterns of thought become chains that bind them to lives of inactivity, poverty, and limitation. Learn to *think big!* Your brain cells are aching for exercise in big thinking. Consider the limitations of thought in

those people you know. Most of them are in positions where they make a limited income and they are doing nothing to change their mode of thought or life. Samuel Johnson said: "The true, strong, and sound mind is the mind that can embrace equally great things and small."

3. **Gather as much knowledge as you can consciously—then let your subconscious take over.** Most people make too much effort to do the really big things of life. They seem to feel, somehow, that they have to do the actual work. Stop and ask yourself what power it is within you that does your breathing, that digests your food, that works your mind. You will then realize that the really big things are done for you by your subconscious. To let your subconscious work better for you, gather as much knowledge as you can consciously about the subjects you wish to become expert in, then turn over this mass of material to your subconscious and let it do the work of sorting out, storing, filing, and using the knowledge you have accumulated.

4. **Give yourself a five-year plan for mental growth.** Your mind likes *definiteness*. Give yourself a five-year plan for study, growth, and evolvement. In that time promise yourself a completely new mental viewpoint, new environment, new work, new

friends, a higher income, and better standards of living. Your mind likes such a challenge as this. It will rise to the occasion and give you the mental power you may need to achieve your five-year goal. Do not stop, however, with a five-year plan; keep expanding and changing this plan as the years go on, so that you always have an unfinished symphony of life which you are working to complete. This gives added purposefulness to living. Pick the books you want to study in that five-year plan, the courses you wish to take, the steps you wish to use to set up a new social life, the friends you wish to cultivate. *Do more than just think about these things*; write them down, make a comprehensive list of your plans and aspirations, so you can consult your list frequently and see that you are on the right path.

5. **Create a need in your life for something you want.** Do not vaguely say, "I want more money," "I'd like to visit Europe next year," or "I'd like to get married." These kinds of statements are weak and inconclusive. Everyone thinks such thoughts once in a while. You must create a need in your life for the things you want. If you want more money, *find a need for more money*. What do you want more money for? Be specific and tell yourself what you will do with it. Why do you want to go to Europe?

For fun? For cultural improvement? To meet a rich marriage partner? For relaxation and rest? Have a real need, and keep reaffirming that need, until it crystallizes in your mind as a dynamic demand on the universal life intelligence.

6. **Make your mind do some creative act each day.** Nothing builds latent mental powers so much as each day making your mind do some creative act. You may not see any immediate results in these small creative efforts but you can take my word for it, they will gradually build giant mental power. Victor Herbert wrote music for more than forty years *without winning recognition*, but every day he sat down and courted the creative muse within, writing a little, patiently waiting and perfecting his talents. Forty years later he won his great success with *Babes in Toyland*, and established himself for all time in the light opera and musical comedy field.

7. **When you experience defeats come back and try again.** A muscle grows by repeated exercise; a brain cell grows *only* when you keep trying, thinking, studying to develop your mind. You need persistent and daily mental exercise if you wish to build your mental power to its fullest capacity. Increase your mental capacity by repeating your

efforts over and over, even in the face of seeming defeats. When someone asked the mighty Babe Ruth what he thought about when he stood on the diamond waiting for the pitcher to throw the ball, the great Babe replied, "I think of only one thing; of hitting the ball!" Your mind must have this persistent and determined feeling about the goal you are trying to achieve.

8. **Accept no limitation on your mental powers.** This priceless ingredient of our Million Dollar Secret is vitally important. Many times it is not the knowledge, the talent, the greatness that a person possesses that brings him success, fame, and fortune. A little talent will go a long way if a person refuses to accept limitations on his abilities.

9. **Organize your thinking by organizing your life.** Order and harmony are God's first laws for creation. If you live in a constant state of confusion and disorder, you cannot have an orderly mind. You can begin today to organize your thinking. You start by first organizing your life. Have a daily schedule and organized surroundings. This will help you acquire the habit of neat and orderly thinking, and your mind will soon release power to do these things in an easier manner than if left to haphazard chance.

10. **Be inspired by noble emotions and high ideals.** No person has ever achieved great heights who was not first inspired by noble emotions and high ideals. Absorb great works of art, writing, and music—read inspiring biographies and emulate their examples. Create beauty and greatness.

Chapter Ten

Become a Receiving Station for Great Ideas

There is a saying in philosophy, "As above, so below." This means that the microcosm, man, reflects all the processes and creative principles that exist in the macrocosm, or the larger universe. Microcosm relates to an organism, regarded as a world in miniature. Man is actually a world in miniature, and he reflects in all his mental and physical processes, all the universal processes of growth, attraction, reproduction, and refinement. The seedling of reality is in man's own mind; his mind is where he creates the world in which he lives.

Once you understand this principle, you will know that part of the Million Dollar Secret lies hidden in your mind as the creative power that every person has locked within his own human consciousness.

There is a picture or pattern within your mind, which has its counterpart in Universal Intelligence—the same intelligence that creates the rose and the oak tree. There is only one major difference between use of this Creative Power within your mind and that in nature: You, being a creature of volition and choice, *may choose the pictures you wish to create in the outer world*, whereas animals, birds, insects, and growing organisms in nature are *forced to create according to a set pattern*.

What one man has thought, experienced, or done may be the common property of all creative minds. You can reflect the knowledge of all the great minds since the beginning of time. Just as all chicks within the hen's egg know how to peck their way out of the shell, so too, your Creative Intelligence knows how to work out all your problems, knows how to give you the ideas and inspiration to make your dreams come true.

You can become a receiving station for great ideas, just as the famous men of history did. You can unlock the creative power of this higher mind within you, just as Napoleon did, as Michelangelo did in his creative masterpieces of marble and canvas. The power that was used by Lincoln, Columbus, Newton, Edison, Washington, and Benjamin Franklin is a part of your own higher consciousness. You may tap the creative mind within and receive from it all the inspiration you need to build your future destiny in the pattern of greatness and genius.

Here is how to use this method to become a receiving station for great ideas:

1. Each night before going to bed spend a few moments picturing in your mind's eye the things you want to achieve, the things you wish to attract, the qualities and talents you want for your own, and even the people you want in your life. Feel that these things are already in existence awaiting your joyous discovery.

2. Ask the "Father Within" to point the way to right work, to the finding or making of the money you need to pay your debts; to the knowledge you need to get a better salary; to the finding of lost or hidden objects. The great ESP researcher Dr. J.B. Rhine tells in his book *Extra-Sensory Perception* of how a girl, whose father had died, needed money desperately. She dreamed one night that her father came to her and told her to look in the secret compartment of an antique dresser. She found it, and stuffed in there were many big bills. How was this knowledge conveyed? Telepathy? Spiritualism? Vibration? Science does not yet know, but there is something at work in another dimension of the universe, which seems to represent a higher mind.

Put your problems to this higher mind within, ask for a solution, and then quietly go to sleep confident that the answer will come to you, either in a dream or when you awaken.

3. If you wish to pick up thoughts of greatness, such as those that inspired the geniuses of the past, sit quietly in your room alone, and meditate on the great person whose imagination you wish to contact. If it is Beethoven, hold his name in your mind; acquire as much knowledge as you can of his life; be conversant with his great music; then sit and wait for the highest inspiration to come through to you. Do the same with any great figure: a scientist, inventor, or business success.

4. You can convey messages to others through this process of speaking to the higher mind within you. Tell the higher mind what you want to convey; hold the name and face of the person in mind; then talk to them as you would if they were there in person. You can also receive mental messages from others through this same process of concentration and visualization. Hold in mind the face of the person you wish to receive messages from; concentrate your mind on that person for a while, and then sit perfectly still and wait and see what thoughts come into your mind.

CHAPTER ELEVEN

How to Seek and Win the Aid of Important People

You've heard the saying, "Nothing succeeds like success." Also, "Money seeks out money." It is true, if you wish to win fame and fortune, you can seldom do it on your own. You must seek out the aid of wealthy and important people.

The Quaker father advised his daughter, "Marry thee not for money, but go thee where money is."

The working of the law of proximity is influential in the lives of many people who have achieved success in their chosen profession. It isn't so much *what* they know as *whom* they know. This has become a cliché in American business, but is nevertheless true. Few of the great geniuses in history could have possibly succeeded without the aid of others.

Edison was a great inventor, but his inventions would have been worthless to the world if they *had not been marketed*. Ford had a great idea in building his horseless carriage, but he needed capital and backing before he could mass-produce his motorcar. Raphael and Michelangelo created great masterpieces in art but they needed their reigning princes of state and church, and the aid of influential, wealthy men and women to give them the means to achieve their great works of art.

It is said, "A man is known through the company he keeps." Most people achieve greatness through reflection. It is just as easy in life to choose the company of friends who are important, politically powerful, creatively active, and wealthy, as to associate with people who are shabby, disorderly in their thinking, lazy, disreputable, shiftless, and negative.

It is important, in building your future career, to choose friends who are striving for the same goals as you; or people who *have already achieved these goals*. It is just as easy to form friendships with people who are going places as to select those who are doomed by their negative habits to failure.

"Hitch your wagon to a star" is a saying that applies to the forming of friendships. Everyone you admit into your life on a close, personal basis should measure up to certain standards. Ask yourself:

- Will our friendship by mutually good?
- What have I to offer this person, and what has he to give?
- Does he have habits that are negative and that might impede my course in life?
- Are his standards high?
- Have I anything to learn from my association with this friend?

It is not selfish for you to be concerned about these new associations, for if you see a person more than three times, he has the power to change your life. You want to be sure that, given such tremendous power, these new friends will change your life for the better.

So many people plan every detail of their lives carefully, and yet completely ignore their social lives. More business is done over cocktails and on golf courses than in offices. It is true that very often, important, busy executives snatch these opportunities of relaxation and conviviality to discuss business matters and make important decisions. Take advantage of this psychological fact. It is easier after a businessman has had a few drinks and eaten a good meal to get his attention than it is to go to his office and get through a retinue of assistants and secretaries.

I recall two meetings with noted authors that came about in such relaxed surroundings in my own career.

One was the great humorist, Irvin Cobb, who was a guest of honor at a luncheon I attended. The other was Rupert Hughes, a great American writer, who I met at a party. Because he was slightly deaf and wore a hearing aid, many people found it difficult to talk to the noted author. I made it a special point to speak distinctly and loudly when addressing him, keeping my face turned towards him so he could read my lips. I spent an instructive and pleasant hour in his company, and when the evening was over, he invited me to lunch, and at another time to play golf with him at the Lakeside Country Club near Hollywood. At the club that day alone, Mr. Hughes introduced me to some of the biggest directors, producers, and stars who later helped my career immeasurably. I was then in my early twenties, and *such contacts would have been impossible without the aid of a well-known and important person.*

Use these secrets for winning the aid of important people:

1. Offer your services and aid to civic betterment groups in your community. Here you will meet people who are in key positions and who can help you immeasurably in achieving your goal.

2. Become affiliated with your local political groups, for they have prestige and power. Many a man has started as a lowly assistant in a political ward, and

risen to a position of power and prominence. You can meet lawyers, judges, and those who are big in politics, and through their aid and influence you can be selected to big-paying jobs.

3. Join a veteran's group, or the American Legion, if you qualify, or any other group that is active in your community. Not only does this pave the way to social activity, but it can lead to an expansion of your business contacts and a position of prestige.

4. Get in the habit of writing to important people, suggesting ideas for the betterment of the community, or offering your help in some charitable work being undertaken. Occasionally write a letter praising the official, and he will definitely take note of you. I have known people who got in to see the heads of some of the biggest businesses in the country through this practice.

5. Use your vacation time profitably. Plan your vacation so that you come in contact with people who might prove valuable to your career.

6. Do not be afraid to present your ideas to important business executives or wealthy people. They are constantly searching for new ideas, new talent, new markets. If you bring them an idea that changes their business for the better, you may work yourself right into an important position. I know one

young man who sent a suggestion to the Canadian Pacific Railroad president for ways of increasing tourist riders, and the president instantly arranged an interview that led the young man to lucrative post.

7. In making contacts with important people, show interest in them and their work. Have respect for their advice and opinions. They have risen in their profession because of specialized skills; respect their judgment.

8. Build the other person's ego, for if he *is* important he will appreciate recognition of that fact. Even great people have their low moments.

9. When you meet people who are important and who might prove helpful, find a common ground of interest, which you can use as a basis for a friendship. This might be work you have in common, school friends you both know, a sport that you can share, and so on.

10. Try to discuss things that are pleasant and non-controversial. Avoid politics and religion. You are judged by the things you talk about.

11. Package your personality so it shows your best side. This means you should have a pleasant, affable, and relaxed personality, one that is easy to get along with. Practice smiling, and learn how to have a

good, hearty laugh, for a good laugh is infectious and often helps win friends. Everyone wants to laugh; no one really wants to share your sad experiences and cry.

12. Give freely of yourself, if you wish to attract and hold the interest of important people. If you have nothing else of value to give the world, give yourself, your interest, your enthusiasm, your charm, your attention, your consideration, and, *most important of all*, your sincere friendship.

CHAPTER TWELVE

Take These Seven Steps Up the Ladder of Success

There is a formula for success that is as definite as the laws that govern mathematics. Success consists of several different component parts, and these are as absolute as the law of gravity.

STEP 1. THE DESIRE TO ACHIEVE

We have spoken elsewhere of desire, but in connection with achieving success, it is vitally important that you use this Emotion of Desire correctly. Everyone wants to succeed. Everyone wants fame and fortune. What you must do is *define exactly the type of success you desire.* The concrete image must exist in your mind first. It is the pattern by which Universal Intelligence can cut the cloth to make the suit you have chosen.

STEP 2. YOUR DREAM OR INNER VISION

All outward forms of creation in the world began with a dream or inner vision. Everyone has some kind of dream of the world in which he wishes to live. This dream resides in the mind, and is instilled by our early childhood thoughts and experiences. You played house, and expressed the idea of love and marriage and having your own family some day. You played doctor and had the dream of someday being one in real life. Dreams crystalize into reality when you apply this formula correctly. It has been said that an idea, when it comes with the force of revelation, will lead to a revolution in your life. The overpowering *idea you hold in your mind* about the life you wish to lead is *the dream or inner vision* that will shape your entire future. You must have this dream firmly fixed and never stray from it.

STEP 3. RELEASE CREATIVE IMAGINATION

Literally, imagination means the act or power of forming mental images of what is not present. It is also the act or power of creating new ideas by combining previous experiences. Creative Intelligence carries you a step further, however, than just forming mental images; it means to cause to come into existence, to make or originate, to cause, to produce, to bring about. When you creatively imagine something you are actually causing it to come into being, for you are *forming it first in your own mind*.

STEP 4. THE POWER OF CONCENTRATION

A lightening bolt can split a giant oak tree because of its concentrated power. The power of concentration is terrific when released in your mind. Most people scatter their mental energy and force by spending ninety percent of their time in thinking over past defeats and disappointments. Their minds spend hours dwelling on the negative aspects of their lives: the failures, the tragedies, the sicknesses, the lost investments. This tendency to concentrate on the negative aspects of life only helps to inscribe these things deeper into the workings of the brain. In using the positive power of concentration, learn to reverse your failures, not to rehearse them, which only tends to make them more real in your mind.

STEP 5. THE POWER OF INTUITION

The humming bird needs no instructor in the art of constructing his thistle-down-lined, swinging nest. Something within him *knows how to construct it perfectly!* The ant requires no one to tell him how to organize his nest and build an anthill. This is an intuitive function within his mind. Emerson spoke of this Intuitive Mind Within in these brilliant words:

> *A man should learn to detect and watch that gleam of light which flashes across his mind from within, more than the lustre of the firmament of bards and sages. Yet, he dismisses without notice his thought, because it is his. In every work of genius we recognize our own rejected thoughts; they come back to us with a certain alienated majesty. Trust thyself; every heart vibrates to that iron string.*

STEP 6. HABIT PATTERNS OF SUCCESS

Study the following questions carefully, for each is a key to the building of new habit patterns of success:

- Are you efficient?
- Are you punctual?
- Are you honest?
- Do you give full value?
- Are you positive?
- Are you confident?
- Are you thrifty?
- Do you know how to handle money?
- Are you able to organize people?

- Are you outgoing in your personality?
- Are you orderly, clean, neat?
- Do you recognize big ideas?
- Do you persist in the face of obstacles?
- Do you believe in yourself?
- Do you think and talk only success?

STEP 7. FAITH IN YOUR DESTINY

Faith in yourself and faith in your destiny—this is an essential step in your climb up the ladder of success. Many talented people never make it because they do not possess this essential ingredient of the Million Dollar Secret.

The twentieth-century novelist Howard Fast wrote a book some years ago. He sent it out to several publishers. They all turned it down. No one had faith in it. Fast had such faith in the ultimate success of the book that he raised $1,000 and published it himself. Only a few hundred copies existed, and undoubtedly, for a time, for a very small sum, anyone could have bought the movie rights.

Then one day a producer read the book, and offered Fast a large sum for the movie rights. *Spartacus* was the name of the book that Howard Fast had faith in. It became one of the great motion pictures of its time, and also smashed the infamous Hollywood blacklist.

Faith in yourself is the "open sesame" to riches and fame. It matters not that others lack faith in you or your works; if you really believe in yourself and your talents, you will build inspiration and power to persist until you have achieved your life goal.

"All things are possible to him that believeth."

About the Authors

Born in 1908 in Upstate New York, ANTHONY NOR-VELL was a popular writer on occult and esoteric topics, particularly the uses of visualization and mind metaphysics. He lectured widely on both coasts, including weekly talks at New York's Carnegie Hall. *The Million Dollar Secret Hidden in Your Mind*, originally published in 1963, is his most popular and enduring book. He died in 1990.

MITCH HOROWITZ, who abridged and introduced this volume, is the PEN Award-winning author of books including *Occult America* and *The Miracle Club: How Thoughts Become Reality*. *The Washington Post* says Mitch "treats esoteric ideas and movements with an even-handed intellectual studiousness that is too often lost in today's raised-voice discussions." Follow him @MitchHorowitz.

www.ingramcontent.com/pod-product-compliance
Lightning Source LLC
Jackson TN
JSHW011942131224
75386JS00041B/1519

* 9 7 8 1 7 2 2 5 0 0 4 4 3 *